50 Pasta Perfection Cooking Recipes

By: Kelly Johnson

Table of Contents

- Spaghetti Carbonara
- Penne alla Vodka
- Fettuccine Alfredo
- Lasagna Bolognese
- Pesto Genovese with Linguine
- Ravioli with Ricotta and Spinach
- Mac and Cheese
- Tagliatelle with Truffle Oil
- Spaghetti Aglio e Olio
- Ziti with Sausage and Peppers
- Shrimp Scampi with Angel Hair
- Pasta Primavera
- Tortellini in Brodo
- Pappardelle with Wild Mushroom Sauce
- Cacio e Pepe
- Gnocchi with Brown Butter Sage Sauce
- Baked Ziti with Ricotta
- Baked Penne with Meatballs
- Spaghetti Puttanesca
- Eggplant Parmesan with Spaghetti
- Orecchiette with Broccoli Rabe and Sausage
- Pasta alla Norma
- Fettuccine with Lemon Cream Sauce
- Bucatini all'Amatriciana
- Lasagna with Spinach and Ricotta
- Macaroni with Beef and Tomato Sauce
- Fregola Sarda with Clams
- Stuffed Shells with Marinara
- Spaghetti with Clams and White Wine Sauce
- Butternut Squash Ravioli with Sage Butter
- Pesto Pasta Salad
- Ravioli with Brown Butter and Parmesan
- Chicken Parmesan with Spaghetti
- Pasta with Roasted Red Pepper Sauce
- Pasta e Fagioli

- Fettuccine with Shrimp and Asparagus
- Linguine with Lobster Sauce
- Sweet Potato Gnocchi with Garlic Butter Sauce
- Pasta with Tuna and Capers
- Penne with Tomato Basil Sauce
- Penne alla Caprese
- Pasta alla Gricia
- Spaghetti with Meat Sauce
- Roasted Tomato and Ricotta Pasta
- Carbonara with Peas
- Tortellini Alfredo
- Spaghetti with Roasted Garlic and Parmesan
- Shrimp and Pesto Stuffed Shells
- Spaghetti with Zucchini and Garlic
- Baked Rigatoni with Mozzarella and Basil

Spaghetti Carbonara

Ingredients:

- 400g spaghetti
- 150g pancetta or guanciale, diced
- 4 large eggs
- 1/2 cup grated Pecorino Romano cheese
- 1/2 cup grated Parmesan cheese
- Freshly ground black pepper
- Salt, for pasta water

Instructions:

1. **Cook the Pasta:**
    - Cook spaghetti in salted boiling water according to package instructions until al dente.
2. **Prepare the Sauce:**
    - While pasta cooks, sauté pancetta or guanciale in a pan until crispy.
3. **Mix Eggs and Cheese:**
    - In a bowl, whisk together eggs, Pecorino Romano, Parmesan, and a generous amount of black pepper.
4. **Combine Pasta and Sauce:**
    - Drain pasta, reserving some cooking water. Toss pasta with pancetta in the pan, then pour egg and cheese mixture over the pasta, stirring quickly to create a creamy sauce. Add reserved pasta water if needed.
5. **Serve:**
    - Serve immediately with extra cheese and pepper.

Penne alla Vodka

Ingredients:

- 400g penne pasta
- 1/2 cup vodka
- 1 can (400g) crushed tomatoes
- 1/2 cup heavy cream
- 1 small onion, chopped
- 2 cloves garlic, minced
- 2 tablespoons olive oil
- 1/4 teaspoon red pepper flakes
- Salt and pepper to taste
- Fresh basil, for garnish
- Parmesan cheese, for serving

Instructions:

1. **Cook the Pasta:**
   - Cook penne in salted water until al dente. Reserve 1/2 cup pasta water.
2. **Prepare the Sauce:**
   - Heat olive oil in a pan, sauté onions and garlic until soft. Add red pepper flakes, vodka, and cook for 2 minutes. Add crushed tomatoes, salt, and pepper, simmer for 10 minutes.
3. **Finish the Sauce:**
   - Stir in heavy cream and cook for another 5 minutes.
4. **Combine Pasta and Sauce:**
   - Toss pasta with sauce, adding reserved pasta water if needed. Garnish with fresh basil and Parmesan.
5. **Serve:**
   - Serve immediately.

Fettuccine Alfredo

Ingredients:

- 400g fettuccine pasta
- 1/2 cup unsalted butter
- 1 cup heavy cream
- 1 1/2 cups grated Parmesan cheese
- 1/4 teaspoon garlic powder (optional)
- Freshly ground black pepper
- Salt for pasta water

Instructions:

1. **Cook the Pasta:**
   - Cook fettuccine in salted boiling water until al dente. Reserve some pasta water.
2. **Make the Sauce:**
   - In a large pan, melt butter over medium heat. Add heavy cream and bring to a simmer. Cook for 5 minutes until slightly thickened.
3. **Add Cheese and Season:**
   - Stir in Parmesan cheese, garlic powder (if using), salt, and pepper. Stir until creamy.
4. **Combine Pasta and Sauce:**
   - Add cooked pasta to the sauce, tossing to coat, adding pasta water if needed to reach desired consistency.
5. **Serve:**
   - Serve immediately with extra Parmesan.

Lasagna Bolognese

Ingredients:

- 12 lasagna noodles
- 1 lb ground beef or pork
- 1 onion, chopped
- 2 cloves garlic, minced
- 2 cups marinara sauce
- 1/2 cup red wine
- 1 cup ricotta cheese
- 2 cups mozzarella cheese, shredded
- 1/2 cup Parmesan cheese, grated
- 1 tablespoon olive oil
- 1 teaspoon dried oregano
- Salt and pepper

Instructions:

1. **Prepare the Bolognese Sauce:**
   - Heat olive oil in a pan, sauté onions and garlic. Add ground meat and brown. Stir in marinara sauce, red wine, oregano, salt, and pepper. Simmer for 20-30 minutes.
2. **Prepare the Noodles:**
   - Cook lasagna noodles according to package instructions. Drain and set aside.
3. **Assemble the Lasagna:**
   - Preheat oven to 375°F (190°C). In a baking dish, spread a layer of Bolognese sauce, followed by noodles, ricotta cheese, mozzarella, and Parmesan. Repeat the layers, finishing with cheese.
4. **Bake:**
   - Cover with foil and bake for 25 minutes, then remove foil and bake for another 10 minutes until bubbly and golden.
5. **Serve:**
   - Let rest for 10 minutes before serving.

Pesto Genovese with Linguine

Ingredients:

- 400g linguine pasta
- 1 cup fresh basil leaves
- 1/4 cup pine nuts
- 1/2 cup Parmesan cheese, grated
- 1/4 cup extra virgin olive oil
- 2 cloves garlic
- Salt and pepper to taste

Instructions:

1. **Cook the Pasta:**
   - Cook linguine in salted boiling water until al dente. Reserve 1/2 cup pasta water.
2. **Make the Pesto:**
   - In a blender or food processor, combine basil, pine nuts, garlic, Parmesan, olive oil, salt, and pepper. Blend until smooth, adding reserved pasta water as needed.
3. **Combine Pasta and Pesto:**
   - Toss the pasta with pesto, adding more pasta water if necessary to coat evenly.
4. **Serve:**
   - Serve immediately with extra Parmesan.

Ravioli with Ricotta and Spinach

Ingredients:

- 1 package ravioli (ricotta and spinach)
- 2 tablespoons butter
- 1 clove garlic, minced
- 1/4 cup fresh sage leaves
- 1/4 cup Parmesan cheese, grated

Instructions:

1. **Cook the Ravioli:**
    - Cook ravioli according to package instructions. Drain and set aside.
2. **Prepare the Sauce:**
    - In a pan, melt butter over medium heat. Add garlic and sage, cooking for 1-2 minutes until fragrant.
3. **Combine Ravioli and Sauce:**
    - Toss cooked ravioli in the pan with the butter and sage sauce.
4. **Serve:**
    - Serve immediately with grated Parmesan.

Mac and Cheese

Ingredients:

- 400g elbow macaroni
- 2 cups shredded cheddar cheese
- 1/2 cup milk
- 1/4 cup butter
- 1 tablespoon all-purpose flour
- 1/2 cup breadcrumbs (optional)
- Salt and pepper to taste

Instructions:

1. **Cook the Macaroni:**
    - Cook macaroni in salted boiling water until al dente. Drain and set aside.
2. **Make the Cheese Sauce:**
    - In a pan, melt butter, then add flour to make a roux. Slowly whisk in milk, then stir in cheese until melted and smooth. Season with salt and pepper.
3. **Combine and Serve:**
    - Stir cooked macaroni into the cheese sauce. Top with breadcrumbs if desired and serve immediately.

Tagliatelle with Truffle Oil

Ingredients:

- 400g tagliatelle pasta
- 1 tablespoon truffle oil
- 2 tablespoons butter
- 1/4 cup Parmesan cheese, grated
- Fresh parsley, chopped
- Salt and pepper to taste

Instructions:

1. **Cook the Pasta:**
    - Cook tagliatelle in salted boiling water until al dente. Reserve 1/2 cup pasta water.
2. **Make the Sauce:**
    - In a pan, melt butter over medium heat. Add truffle oil and season with salt and pepper.
3. **Combine Pasta and Sauce:**
    - Toss cooked tagliatelle in the pan with the truffle butter sauce, adding reserved pasta water if needed.
4. **Serve:**
    - Serve immediately with grated Parmesan and fresh parsley.

Spaghetti Aglio e Olio

Ingredients:

- 400g spaghetti
- 6 cloves garlic, thinly sliced
- 1/4 cup extra virgin olive oil
- 1/2 teaspoon red pepper flakes
- Fresh parsley, chopped
- Salt for pasta water
- Freshly ground black pepper
- Parmesan cheese (optional)

Instructions:

1. **Cook the Pasta:**
   - Cook spaghetti in salted boiling water until al dente. Reserve 1/2 cup pasta water.
2. **Make the Sauce:**
   - Heat olive oil in a pan over medium heat. Add sliced garlic and red pepper flakes. Cook until garlic is golden and fragrant, being careful not to burn it.
3. **Combine Pasta and Sauce:**
   - Add cooked spaghetti to the pan, tossing it in the garlic oil. Add reserved pasta water to help coat the pasta evenly.
4. **Serve:**
   - Garnish with chopped parsley and black pepper. Optionally, sprinkle with Parmesan cheese before serving.

Ziti with Sausage and Peppers

Ingredients:

- 400g ziti pasta
- 1 lb Italian sausage, removed from casing
- 1 red bell pepper, sliced
- 1 green bell pepper, sliced
- 1 onion, sliced
- 2 cloves garlic, minced
- 1 can (400g) crushed tomatoes
- 1/4 cup fresh basil, chopped
- Olive oil for cooking
- Salt and pepper to taste

Instructions:

1. **Cook the Pasta:**
   - Cook ziti in salted boiling water until al dente. Drain and set aside.
2. **Cook the Sausage:**
   - Heat olive oil in a large pan. Add sausage and cook, breaking it apart, until browned.
3. **Sauté Vegetables:**
   - Add garlic, bell peppers, and onion to the pan. Cook until vegetables are soft.
4. **Add Sauce:**
   - Stir in crushed tomatoes, basil, salt, and pepper. Let it simmer for 10 minutes.
5. **Combine Pasta and Sauce:**
   - Toss cooked ziti into the sauce, mixing until well coated.
6. **Serve:**
   - Serve with extra basil on top.

Shrimp Scampi with Angel Hair

Ingredients:

- 400g angel hair pasta
- 500g shrimp, peeled and deveined
- 4 cloves garlic, minced
- 1/4 cup white wine
- 1/4 cup lemon juice
- 1/4 cup fresh parsley, chopped
- 1/4 teaspoon red pepper flakes (optional)
- 1/4 cup unsalted butter
- Olive oil for cooking
- Salt and pepper to taste

Instructions:

1. **Cook the Pasta:**
    - Cook angel hair pasta in salted boiling water until al dente. Drain and set aside.
2. **Cook the Shrimp:**
    - Heat olive oil in a pan over medium-high heat. Add shrimp and cook until pink. Remove from the pan and set aside.
3. **Make the Sauce:**
    - In the same pan, add garlic and cook for 1 minute. Stir in white wine and lemon juice, scraping up any browned bits from the pan.
4. **Combine Pasta, Shrimp, and Sauce:**
    - Add butter to the sauce and stir until melted. Return shrimp to the pan. Toss in cooked pasta, parsley, and red pepper flakes.
5. **Serve:**
    - Serve immediately, garnished with extra parsley.

Pasta Primavera

Ingredients:

- 400g pasta (penne, fusilli, or spaghetti)
- 1 zucchini, sliced
- 1 yellow bell pepper, sliced
- 1 red bell pepper, sliced
- 1 cup cherry tomatoes, halved
- 2 cloves garlic, minced
- 1/4 cup olive oil
- 1/4 cup Parmesan cheese, grated
- Salt and pepper to taste
- Fresh basil, for garnish

Instructions:

1. **Cook the Pasta:**
    - Cook pasta in salted boiling water until al dente. Drain and set aside.
2. **Sauté the Vegetables:**
    - Heat olive oil in a pan. Add garlic, zucchini, and bell peppers, cooking until vegetables are tender. Add tomatoes and cook for another 2-3 minutes.
3. **Combine Pasta and Vegetables:**
    - Add the cooked pasta to the pan with vegetables. Toss to combine. Season with salt and pepper.
4. **Serve:**
    - Garnish with Parmesan cheese and fresh basil.

Tortellini in Brodo

Ingredients:

- 400g tortellini (fresh or frozen)
- 4 cups chicken or vegetable broth
- 1 small onion, peeled
- 1 carrot, peeled
- 1 celery stalk, chopped
- 1 bay leaf
- Salt and pepper to taste
- Fresh parsley, chopped (optional)

Instructions:

1. **Prepare the Broth:**
    - In a large pot, bring the broth to a simmer. Add the onion, carrot, celery, and bay leaf. Simmer for 20-30 minutes to infuse the flavors.
2. **Cook the Tortellini:**
    - Strain the broth and return it to the pot. Bring it to a boil and add tortellini. Cook according to package instructions.
3. **Serve:**
    - Ladle the tortellini and broth into bowls. Garnish with fresh parsley.

Pappardelle with Wild Mushroom Sauce

Ingredients:

- 400g pappardelle pasta
- 300g mixed wild mushrooms, sliced
- 2 cloves garlic, minced
- 1/2 cup dry white wine
- 1/2 cup heavy cream
- 1/4 cup Parmesan cheese, grated
- 2 tablespoons unsalted butter
- Olive oil for cooking
- Salt and pepper to taste
- Fresh thyme, for garnish

Instructions:

1. **Cook the Pasta:**
   - Cook pappardelle in salted boiling water until al dente. Drain and set aside.
2. **Sauté the Mushrooms:**
   - Heat olive oil and butter in a pan. Add garlic and mushrooms, cooking until soft and golden. Season with salt and pepper.
3. **Make the Sauce:**
   - Pour in white wine and cook until reduced by half. Stir in heavy cream and cook for 2-3 minutes until thickened.
4. **Combine Pasta and Sauce:**
   - Toss cooked pappardelle in the mushroom sauce. Add Parmesan cheese and mix until creamy.
5. **Serve:**
   - Garnish with fresh thyme and serve immediately.

Cacio e Pepe

Ingredients:

- 400g spaghetti or tonnarelli
- 1 1/2 cups Pecorino Romano cheese, grated
- 1 teaspoon black pepper, freshly ground
- Salt for pasta water

Instructions:

1. **Cook the Pasta:**
   - Cook pasta in salted boiling water until al dente. Reserve 1/2 cup pasta water.
2. **Prepare the Sauce:**
   - In a large pan, toast black pepper over medium heat for 1-2 minutes until fragrant.
3. **Combine Pasta and Sauce:**
   - Add cooked pasta to the pan with the toasted pepper. Stir in Pecorino Romano, adding reserved pasta water until the sauce is creamy and coats the pasta.
4. **Serve:**
   - Serve immediately with extra cheese.

Gnocchi with Brown Butter Sage Sauce

Ingredients:

- 500g potato gnocchi (fresh or frozen)
- 1/4 cup unsalted butter
- 12 fresh sage leaves
- 1/4 cup Parmesan cheese, grated
- Salt and pepper to taste

Instructions:

1. **Cook the Gnocchi:**
   - Cook gnocchi in salted boiling water until they float to the surface. Drain and set aside.
2. **Make the Sauce:**
   - In a pan, melt butter over medium heat. Add sage leaves and cook until the butter becomes golden brown and aromatic, about 2-3 minutes.
3. **Combine Gnocchi and Sauce:**
   - Add cooked gnocchi to the pan, tossing them in the brown butter sauce until well coated.
4. **Serve:**
   - Sprinkle with Parmesan cheese and season with salt and pepper before serving.

Baked Ziti with Ricotta

Ingredients:

- 400g ziti pasta
- 1 jar (24oz) marinara sauce
- 1 1/2 cups ricotta cheese
- 1 1/2 cups mozzarella cheese, shredded
- 1/2 cup Parmesan cheese, grated
- 1 egg
- 2 teaspoons dried basil
- Salt and pepper to taste
- Olive oil for greasing

Instructions:

1. **Cook the Pasta:**
    - Cook ziti in salted boiling water until al dente. Drain and set aside.
2. **Prepare the Ricotta Mixture:**
    - In a bowl, mix ricotta, egg, basil, and half of the Parmesan cheese. Season with salt and pepper.
3. **Assemble the Dish:**
    - Preheat the oven to 375°F (190°C). Grease a baking dish with olive oil. Layer pasta, marinara sauce, ricotta mixture, and mozzarella cheese in the dish.
4. **Bake:**
    - Sprinkle the remaining Parmesan cheese over the top. Bake for 25-30 minutes until bubbly and golden.
5. **Serve:**
    - Let it cool slightly before serving.

Baked Penne with Meatballs

Ingredients:

- 400g penne pasta
- 1 jar (24oz) marinara sauce
- 12-15 meatballs (store-bought or homemade)
- 1 1/2 cups mozzarella cheese, shredded
- 1/2 cup Parmesan cheese, grated
- 1/4 cup fresh basil, chopped
- Salt and pepper to taste

Instructions:

1. **Cook the Pasta:**
    - Cook penne in salted boiling water until al dente. Drain and set aside.
2. **Prepare the Meatballs:**
    - Cook meatballs in marinara sauce until heated through.
3. **Assemble the Dish:**
    - Preheat the oven to 375°F (190°C). Grease a baking dish. Layer cooked penne, marinara sauce with meatballs, and mozzarella cheese.
4. **Bake:**
    - Sprinkle with Parmesan cheese and bake for 20-25 minutes, until cheese is melted and bubbly.
5. **Serve:**
    - Garnish with fresh basil before serving.

Spaghetti Puttanesca

Ingredients:

- 400g spaghetti
- 1/4 cup olive oil
- 4 cloves garlic, minced
- 1 can (14oz) diced tomatoes
- 1/4 cup Kalamata olives, pitted and chopped
- 2 tablespoons capers, rinsed
- 1/2 teaspoon red pepper flakes
- Salt and pepper to taste
- Fresh parsley, chopped

Instructions:

1. **Cook the Pasta:**
    - Cook spaghetti in salted boiling water until al dente. Drain and set aside.
2. **Make the Sauce:**
    - Heat olive oil in a pan over medium heat. Add garlic and cook until fragrant. Stir in diced tomatoes, olives, capers, red pepper flakes, salt, and pepper. Simmer for 10 minutes.
3. **Combine Pasta and Sauce:**
    - Toss cooked spaghetti in the sauce until well coated.
4. **Serve:**
    - Garnish with fresh parsley and serve.

Eggplant Parmesan with Spaghetti

Ingredients:

- 2 medium eggplants, sliced
- 2 cups marinara sauce
- 2 cups mozzarella cheese, shredded
- 1/2 cup Parmesan cheese, grated
- 2 eggs, beaten
- 1 cup breadcrumbs
- 1/4 cup fresh basil, chopped
- 400g spaghetti
- Olive oil for frying

Instructions:

1. **Prepare the Eggplant:**
    - Preheat the oven to 375°F (190°C). Dip eggplant slices in beaten eggs, then coat in breadcrumbs. Fry in olive oil until golden and crispy. Drain on paper towels.
2. **Cook the Pasta:**
    - Cook spaghetti in salted boiling water until al dente. Drain and set aside.
3. **Assemble the Dish:**
    - In a baking dish, layer eggplant slices, marinara sauce, mozzarella, and Parmesan. Repeat layers and top with cheese.
4. **Bake:**
    - Bake for 25-30 minutes until bubbly and golden.
5. **Serve:**
    - Serve with spaghetti and fresh basil on top.

Orecchiette with Broccoli Rabe and Sausage

Ingredients:

- 400g orecchiette pasta
- 2 links Italian sausage, casings removed
- 1 bunch broccoli rabe, trimmed and chopped
- 2 cloves garlic, minced
- 1/4 teaspoon red pepper flakes
- 1/4 cup Parmesan cheese, grated
- Olive oil for cooking
- Salt and pepper to taste

Instructions:

1. **Cook the Pasta:**
    - Cook orecchiette in salted boiling water until al dente. Drain, reserving some pasta water.
2. **Cook the Sausage:**
    - In a large pan, cook sausage until browned, breaking it into pieces. Remove from the pan.
3. **Sauté the Vegetables:**
    - In the same pan, heat olive oil. Add garlic and red pepper flakes. Sauté until fragrant. Add broccoli rabe and cook until wilted.
4. **Combine Pasta and Sauce:**
    - Add cooked orecchiette and sausage to the pan. Toss everything together, adding reserved pasta water if needed.
5. **Serve:**
    - Sprinkle with Parmesan cheese and serve.

Pasta alla Norma

Ingredients:

- 400g pasta (rigatoni or spaghetti)
- 2 medium eggplants, diced
- 2 cups marinara sauce
- 1/4 cup fresh basil, chopped
- 1/2 cup ricotta salata cheese, grated
- Olive oil for frying
- Salt and pepper to taste

Instructions:

1. **Cook the Pasta:**
    - Cook pasta in salted boiling water until al dente. Drain and set aside.
2. **Fry the Eggplant:**
    - Heat olive oil in a pan. Fry eggplant pieces until golden and crispy. Drain on paper towels.
3. **Make the Sauce:**
    - In a separate pan, heat marinara sauce and stir in fried eggplant. Simmer for 5 minutes.
4. **Combine Pasta and Sauce:**
    - Toss cooked pasta in the sauce until well coated.
5. **Serve:**
    - Top with ricotta salata and fresh basil.

Fettuccine with Lemon Cream Sauce

Ingredients:

- 400g fettuccine pasta
- 1/2 cup heavy cream
- 1/4 cup lemon juice
- 1 tablespoon lemon zest
- 1/4 cup Parmesan cheese, grated
- 2 tablespoons unsalted butter
- Salt and pepper to taste
- Fresh parsley, chopped

Instructions:

1. **Cook the Pasta:**
    - Cook fettuccine in salted boiling water until al dente. Drain, reserving some pasta water.
2. **Make the Sauce:**
    - In a pan, melt butter over medium heat. Stir in cream, lemon juice, and zest. Simmer for 2-3 minutes until thickened. Add Parmesan cheese, salt, and pepper.
3. **Combine Pasta and Sauce:**
    - Toss cooked fettuccine in the sauce, adding reserved pasta water to adjust consistency.
4. **Serve:**
    - Garnish with fresh parsley and serve.

Bucatini all'Amatriciana

Ingredients:

- 400g bucatini pasta
- 150g guanciale or pancetta, diced
- 1 can (14oz) diced tomatoes
- 1/4 teaspoon red pepper flakes
- 1/4 cup Pecorino Romano cheese, grated
- Olive oil for cooking
- Salt and pepper to taste

Instructions:

1. **Cook the Pasta:**
    - Cook bucatini in salted boiling water until al dente. Drain and set aside.
2. **Cook the Guanciale:**
    - In a large pan, heat olive oil and cook guanciale until crispy.
3. **Make the Sauce:**
    - Stir in red pepper flakes and diced tomatoes. Simmer for 10-15 minutes, adjusting with salt and pepper.
4. **Combine Pasta and Sauce:**
    - Toss cooked bucatini in the sauce until well coated.
5. **Serve:**
    - Sprinkle with Pecorino Romano and serve immediately.

Lasagna with Spinach and Ricotta

Ingredients:

- 12 lasagna noodles
- 1 1/2 cups ricotta cheese
- 2 cups cooked spinach, chopped
- 2 cups marinara sauce
- 2 cups mozzarella cheese, shredded
- 1/2 cup Parmesan cheese, grated
- 1 egg
- 1 teaspoon dried oregano
- Salt and pepper to taste
- Olive oil for greasing

Instructions:

1. **Prepare the Noodles:**
   - Cook lasagna noodles according to package instructions. Drain and set aside.
2. **Prepare the Filling:**
   - In a bowl, combine ricotta cheese, spinach, egg, oregano, salt, and pepper.
3. **Assemble the Lasagna:**
   - Preheat the oven to 375°F (190°C). Grease a baking dish. Layer marinara sauce, lasagna noodles, ricotta mixture, and mozzarella. Repeat layers and top with Parmesan cheese.
4. **Bake:**
   - Cover with foil and bake for 25 minutes. Remove foil and bake for an additional 10 minutes, until bubbly and golden.
5. **Serve:**
   - Let it cool for a few minutes before serving.

Macaroni with Beef and Tomato Sauce

Ingredients:

- 400g elbow macaroni
- 1 lb ground beef
- 1 jar (24oz) marinara sauce
- 1/2 onion, chopped
- 2 cloves garlic, minced
- 1 teaspoon dried oregano
- 1/4 cup Parmesan cheese, grated
- Salt and pepper to taste

Instructions:

1. **Cook the Pasta:**
    - Cook elbow macaroni in salted boiling water until al dente. Drain and set aside.
2. **Cook the Beef:**
    - In a large skillet, brown the ground beef with onions and garlic over medium heat. Drain excess fat.
3. **Make the Sauce:**
    - Add marinara sauce and oregano to the beef. Simmer for 10 minutes. Season with salt and pepper.
4. **Combine Pasta and Sauce:**
    - Toss cooked macaroni with the beef sauce mixture until well coated.
5. **Serve:**
    - Sprinkle with Parmesan cheese before serving.

Fregola Sarda with Clams

Ingredients:

- 1 1/2 cups fregola sarda
- 2 lbs clams, cleaned
- 1/4 cup olive oil
- 2 cloves garlic, minced
- 1/2 cup white wine
- 1/2 teaspoon red pepper flakes
- Fresh parsley, chopped
- Lemon wedges for serving
- Salt and pepper to taste

Instructions:

1. **Cook the Fregola:**
   - In salted boiling water, cook fregola sarda until tender. Drain and set aside.
2. **Prepare the Clams:**
   - In a large pan, heat olive oil over medium heat. Add garlic and cook until fragrant. Add clams and white wine. Cover and cook for 5-7 minutes until clams open.
3. **Combine:**
   - Stir in cooked fregola sarda, red pepper flakes, salt, and pepper. Toss everything together.
4. **Serve:**
   - Garnish with fresh parsley and lemon wedges before serving.

Stuffed Shells with Marinara

Ingredients:

- 20 jumbo pasta shells
- 2 cups ricotta cheese
- 1 1/2 cups mozzarella cheese, shredded
- 1/2 cup Parmesan cheese, grated
- 1 egg
- 1 teaspoon dried basil
- 1 jar (24oz) marinara sauce
- Fresh basil for garnish

Instructions:

1. **Cook the Shells:**
    - Cook jumbo shells according to package instructions. Drain and set aside.
2. **Prepare the Filling:**
    - In a bowl, combine ricotta cheese, 1 cup mozzarella, Parmesan, egg, basil, salt, and pepper.
3. **Assemble the Dish:**
    - Preheat the oven to 375°F (190°C). Stuff each shell with the ricotta mixture and arrange them in a baking dish. Pour marinara sauce over the shells and top with remaining mozzarella.
4. **Bake:**
    - Cover with foil and bake for 25 minutes. Remove foil and bake for an additional 10 minutes.
5. **Serve:**
    - Garnish with fresh basil before serving.

Spaghetti with Clams and White Wine Sauce

Ingredients:

- 400g spaghetti
- 2 lbs clams, cleaned
- 1/4 cup olive oil
- 4 cloves garlic, minced
- 1/2 cup white wine
- Fresh parsley, chopped
- 1/2 teaspoon red pepper flakes
- Salt and pepper to taste

Instructions:

1. **Cook the Pasta:**
   - Cook spaghetti in salted boiling water until al dente. Drain, reserving some pasta water.
2. **Prepare the Clams:**
   - In a large pan, heat olive oil over medium heat. Add garlic and cook until fragrant. Add clams and white wine. Cover and cook for 5-7 minutes until clams open.
3. **Combine Pasta and Sauce:**
   - Toss cooked spaghetti with clams, red pepper flakes, salt, and pepper. Add reserved pasta water if necessary.
4. **Serve:**
   - Garnish with fresh parsley and serve.

Butternut Squash Ravioli with Sage Butter

Ingredients:

- 12-15 butternut squash ravioli
- 1/4 cup unsalted butter
- 8-10 fresh sage leaves
- 1/4 cup Parmesan cheese, grated
- Salt and pepper to taste

Instructions:

1. **Cook the Ravioli:**
   - Cook butternut squash ravioli in salted boiling water until tender. Drain and set aside.
2. **Prepare the Sage Butter:**
   - In a pan, melt butter over medium heat. Add sage leaves and cook until crispy, about 2 minutes.
3. **Combine:**
   - Toss cooked ravioli in the sage butter. Season with salt and pepper.
4. **Serve:**
   - Sprinkle with Parmesan cheese before serving.

Pesto Pasta Salad

Ingredients:

- 400g pasta (penne or fusilli)
- 1/2 cup pesto sauce
- 1/2 cup cherry tomatoes, halved
- 1/4 cup Kalamata olives, pitted and chopped
- 1/4 cup mozzarella balls, halved
- Fresh basil leaves for garnish
- Salt and pepper to taste

Instructions:

1. **Cook the Pasta:**
   - Cook pasta in salted boiling water until al dente. Drain and rinse with cold water.
2. **Assemble the Salad:**
   - In a large bowl, toss pasta with pesto sauce, cherry tomatoes, olives, mozzarella, salt, and pepper.
3. **Serve:**
   - Garnish with fresh basil leaves and serve chilled.

Ravioli with Brown Butter and Parmesan

Ingredients:

- 12-15 ravioli (your choice of filling)
- 1/4 cup unsalted butter
- 1/4 teaspoon sage, chopped
- 1/4 cup Parmesan cheese, grated
- Salt and pepper to taste

Instructions:

1. **Cook the Ravioli:**
    - Cook ravioli in salted boiling water until tender. Drain and set aside.
2. **Make the Brown Butter Sauce:**
    - In a pan, melt butter over medium heat. Cook until golden brown and fragrant. Add sage and cook for another minute.
3. **Combine:**
    - Toss cooked ravioli in the brown butter sauce. Season with salt and pepper.
4. **Serve:**
    - Sprinkle with Parmesan cheese and serve.

Chicken Parmesan with Spaghetti

Ingredients:

- 2 chicken breasts, breaded and fried
- 1 jar (24oz) marinara sauce
- 1 1/2 cups mozzarella cheese, shredded
- 1/2 cup Parmesan cheese, grated
- 400g spaghetti
- 1 egg, beaten
- 1 cup breadcrumbs
- Olive oil for frying

Instructions:

1. **Cook the Pasta:**
   - Cook spaghetti in salted boiling water until al dente. Drain and set aside.
2. **Prepare the Chicken:**
   - Dip chicken breasts in beaten egg, then coat in breadcrumbs. Fry in olive oil until golden brown and cooked through.
3. **Assemble the Dish:**
   - Preheat the oven to 375°F (190°C). Place fried chicken in a baking dish. Top with marinara sauce and mozzarella cheese.
4. **Bake:**
   - Bake for 10-15 minutes, until cheese is melted and bubbly.
5. **Serve:**
   - Serve chicken Parmesan with cooked spaghetti and sprinkle with Parmesan cheese.

Pasta with Roasted Red Pepper Sauce

Ingredients:

- 400g pasta (penne or spaghetti)
- 2 large red bell peppers, roasted and peeled
- 2 cloves garlic, minced
- 1/4 cup olive oil
- 1/2 cup heavy cream
- 1/4 cup Parmesan cheese, grated
- Salt and pepper to taste
- Fresh basil for garnish

Instructions:

1. **Roast the Peppers:**
   - Roast the red bell peppers under a broiler or over an open flame until charred. Peel the skins and remove seeds. Blend the peppers into a smooth puree.
2. **Cook the Pasta:**
   - Cook pasta in salted boiling water until al dente. Drain and set aside.
3. **Make the Sauce:**
   - In a pan, heat olive oil and sauté garlic until fragrant. Add the roasted red pepper puree and cook for 5 minutes. Stir in heavy cream and Parmesan cheese, and season with salt and pepper.
4. **Combine:**
   - Toss cooked pasta with the roasted red pepper sauce.
5. **Serve:**
   - Garnish with fresh basil before serving.

Pasta e Fagioli

Ingredients:

- 200g small pasta (ditalini or elbow)
- 2 cans (15oz each) cannellini beans, drained and rinsed
- 1/4 cup olive oil
- 2 cloves garlic, minced
- 1 onion, chopped
- 1 carrot, chopped
- 2 celery stalks, chopped
- 1 can (14oz) crushed tomatoes
- 4 cups vegetable broth
- 1 teaspoon dried oregano
- Salt and pepper to taste
- Fresh parsley for garnish

Instructions:

1. **Cook the Vegetables:**
    - Heat olive oil in a large pot. Sauté garlic, onion, carrot, and celery until softened, about 5 minutes.
2. **Add Tomatoes and Broth:**
    - Add crushed tomatoes, vegetable broth, oregano, salt, and pepper. Bring to a simmer and cook for 15 minutes.
3. **Cook the Pasta:**
    - Add beans and pasta to the pot. Simmer for 10 minutes, until pasta is tender.
4. **Serve:**
    - Garnish with fresh parsley and serve.

Fettuccine with Shrimp and Asparagus

Ingredients:

- 400g fettuccine pasta
- 1 lb shrimp, peeled and deveined
- 1 bunch asparagus, trimmed and cut into pieces
- 1/4 cup olive oil
- 3 cloves garlic, minced
- 1/2 cup white wine
- 1/2 cup heavy cream
- 1/4 cup Parmesan cheese, grated
- Salt and pepper to taste

Instructions:

1. **Cook the Pasta:**
   - Cook fettuccine in salted boiling water until al dente. Drain and set aside.
2. **Cook the Shrimp and Asparagus:**
   - In a large skillet, heat olive oil and sauté garlic until fragrant. Add shrimp and asparagus, cooking until shrimp is pink and asparagus is tender.
3. **Make the Sauce:**
   - Add white wine and simmer for 2-3 minutes. Stir in heavy cream and Parmesan cheese, and season with salt and pepper.
4. **Combine:**
   - Toss cooked pasta with shrimp and asparagus mixture, ensuring everything is coated with the sauce.
5. **Serve:**
   - Serve immediately with extra Parmesan cheese.

Linguine with Lobster Sauce

Ingredients:

- 400g linguine pasta
- 2 lobster tails, cooked and chopped
- 1/4 cup olive oil
- 2 cloves garlic, minced
- 1/2 cup white wine
- 1 cup heavy cream
- 1/4 cup tomato paste
- 1/2 teaspoon red pepper flakes
- Salt and pepper to taste
- Fresh parsley for garnish

Instructions:

1. **Cook the Pasta:**
   - Cook linguine in salted boiling water until al dente. Drain and set aside.
2. **Prepare the Sauce:**
   - In a pan, heat olive oil and sauté garlic until fragrant. Add white wine and simmer for 2-3 minutes. Stir in tomato paste, red pepper flakes, and heavy cream, simmering for another 5 minutes.
3. **Add Lobster:**
   - Stir in chopped lobster meat and cook for 2-3 minutes until heated through.
4. **Combine:**
   - Toss linguine with the lobster sauce. Season with salt and pepper.
5. **Serve:**
   - Garnish with fresh parsley and serve.

Sweet Potato Gnocchi with Garlic Butter Sauce

Ingredients:

- 1 lb sweet potatoes, roasted and mashed
- 1 1/2 cups all-purpose flour
- 1/2 teaspoon salt
- 1 egg
- 1/4 cup unsalted butter
- 3 cloves garlic, minced
- Fresh sage leaves
- Salt and pepper to taste
- Parmesan cheese for garnish

Instructions:

1. **Make the Gnocchi:**
   - In a bowl, combine mashed sweet potatoes, flour, salt, and egg. Mix to form a dough. Roll into small logs and cut into bite-sized pieces. Gently press each piece with a fork to shape.
2. **Cook the Gnocchi:**
   - Boil gnocchi in salted water until they float, about 2-3 minutes. Remove and set aside.
3. **Prepare the Garlic Butter Sauce:**
   - In a pan, melt butter over medium heat. Add garlic and sage leaves, cooking until fragrant and crispy.
4. **Combine:**
   - Toss cooked gnocchi in the garlic butter sauce, seasoning with salt and pepper.
5. **Serve:**
   - Garnish with Parmesan cheese and serve.

Pasta with Tuna and Capers

Ingredients:

- 400g pasta (spaghetti or penne)
- 1 can (5 oz) tuna in olive oil, drained
- 2 tablespoons capers, rinsed
- 1/4 cup olive oil
- 3 cloves garlic, minced
- 1/2 teaspoon red pepper flakes
- Salt and pepper to taste
- Fresh parsley for garnish

Instructions:

1. **Cook the Pasta:**
    - Cook pasta in salted boiling water until al dente. Drain and set aside.
2. **Prepare the Sauce:**
    - In a large skillet, heat olive oil and sauté garlic until fragrant. Add tuna and capers, cooking for 3-4 minutes.
3. **Combine:**
    - Toss cooked pasta with the tuna mixture. Season with red pepper flakes, salt, and pepper.
4. **Serve:**
    - Garnish with fresh parsley and serve.

Penne with Tomato Basil Sauce

Ingredients:

- 400g penne pasta
- 1 can (14oz) crushed tomatoes
- 1/4 cup olive oil
- 2 cloves garlic, minced
- 1 teaspoon dried basil
- Salt and pepper to taste
- Fresh basil leaves for garnish
- Parmesan cheese for serving

Instructions:

1. **Cook the Pasta:**
    - Cook penne in salted boiling water until al dente. Drain and set aside.
2. **Make the Sauce:**
    - In a pan, heat olive oil and sauté garlic until fragrant. Add crushed tomatoes, basil, salt, and pepper, simmering for 10 minutes.
3. **Combine:**
    - Toss cooked penne with the tomato basil sauce.
4. **Serve:**
    - Garnish with fresh basil and Parmesan cheese before serving.

Penne alla Caprese

Ingredients:

- 400g penne pasta
- 2 cups cherry tomatoes, halved
- 1 cup fresh mozzarella balls, halved
- 1/4 cup olive oil
- 2 cloves garlic, minced
- 1/4 cup fresh basil, chopped
- Salt and pepper to taste
- Balsamic glaze for drizzling

Instructions:

1. **Cook the Pasta:**
   - Cook penne in salted boiling water until al dente. Drain and set aside.
2. **Make the Sauce:**
   - In a pan, heat olive oil and sauté garlic until fragrant. Add cherry tomatoes and cook until soft.
3. **Combine:**
   - Toss cooked penne with tomatoes, mozzarella, and fresh basil. Season with salt and pepper.
4. **Serve:**
   - Drizzle with balsamic glaze and serve immediately.

Pasta alla Gricia

Ingredients:

- 400g pasta (rigatoni or spaghetti)
- 4 oz guanciale, diced
- 1/4 cup Pecorino Romano cheese, grated
- 1/4 cup Parmesan cheese, grated
- Fresh ground black pepper to taste

Instructions:

1. **Cook the Pasta:**
    - Cook pasta in salted boiling water until al dente. Drain, reserving some pasta water.
2. **Cook the Guanciale:**
    - In a pan, cook diced guanciale over medium heat until crispy, about 5 minutes.
3. **Make the Sauce:**
    - Add some pasta water to the pan with the guanciale to create a sauce. Toss in the cooked pasta.
4. **Combine:**
    - Stir in Pecorino Romano and Parmesan cheese, adding more pasta water if needed to coat the pasta.
5. **Serve:**
    - Season with fresh black pepper and serve immediately.

Spaghetti with Meat Sauce

Ingredients:

- 400g spaghetti pasta
- 1 lb ground beef
- 1 onion, chopped
- 2 cloves garlic, minced
- 1 can (14oz) crushed tomatoes
- 2 tablespoons tomato paste
- 1 teaspoon dried basil
- 1 teaspoon dried oregano
- Salt and pepper to taste
- Fresh basil for garnish
- Parmesan cheese for serving

Instructions:

1. **Cook the Pasta:**
    - Cook spaghetti in salted boiling water until al dente. Drain and set aside.
2. **Make the Meat Sauce:**
    - In a large pan, cook ground beef until browned. Remove excess fat. Add onion and garlic, cooking until softened. Stir in crushed tomatoes, tomato paste, basil, oregano, salt, and pepper. Simmer for 20 minutes.
3. **Combine:**
    - Toss cooked spaghetti with the meat sauce.
4. **Serve:**
    - Garnish with fresh basil and Parmesan cheese before serving.

Roasted Tomato and Ricotta Pasta

Ingredients:

- 400g pasta (penne or fusilli)
- 4 large tomatoes, halved
- 1 tablespoon olive oil
- 1/2 teaspoon salt
- 1/4 teaspoon black pepper
- 1 cup ricotta cheese
- 1/4 cup fresh basil, chopped
- Parmesan cheese for garnish

Instructions:

1. **Roast the Tomatoes:**
    - Preheat the oven to 400°F (200°C). Place halved tomatoes on a baking sheet, drizzle with olive oil, and season with salt and pepper. Roast for 25-30 minutes until soft.
2. **Cook the Pasta:**
    - Cook pasta in salted boiling water until al dente. Drain and set aside.
3. **Make the Sauce:**
    - In a large bowl, mash the roasted tomatoes. Add ricotta cheese and mix until smooth.
4. **Combine:**
    - Toss the cooked pasta with the tomato-ricotta sauce.
5. **Serve:**
    - Garnish with fresh basil and Parmesan cheese before serving.

Carbonara with Peas

Ingredients:

- 400g spaghetti or fettuccine
- 6 oz pancetta or bacon, chopped
- 2 eggs
- 1/2 cup Parmesan cheese, grated
- 1 cup frozen peas, thawed
- Salt and pepper to taste
- Fresh parsley for garnish

Instructions:

1. **Cook the Pasta:**
   - Cook pasta in salted boiling water until al dente. Reserve 1 cup of pasta water before draining.
2. **Cook the Pancetta:**
   - In a pan, cook pancetta over medium heat until crispy, about 5-7 minutes.
3. **Make the Carbonara Sauce:**
   - In a bowl, whisk together eggs, Parmesan cheese, salt, and pepper.
4. **Combine:**
   - Toss the cooked pasta with pancetta. Add the egg mixture and reserved pasta water, stirring quickly to create a creamy sauce. Fold in peas.
5. **Serve:**
   - Garnish with fresh parsley and serve immediately.

Tortellini Alfredo

Ingredients:

- 400g cheese tortellini (fresh or frozen)
- 1/2 cup unsalted butter
- 2 cloves garlic, minced
- 1 cup heavy cream
- 1 cup Parmesan cheese, grated
- Salt and pepper to taste
- Fresh parsley for garnish

Instructions:

1. **Cook the Tortellini:**
   - Cook tortellini in salted boiling water according to package instructions. Drain and set aside.
2. **Make the Alfredo Sauce:**
   - In a large pan, melt butter over medium heat. Add garlic and sauté for 1 minute. Stir in heavy cream and simmer for 5 minutes. Add Parmesan cheese and stir until melted and smooth. Season with salt and pepper.
3. **Combine:**
   - Toss cooked tortellini in the Alfredo sauce until well coated.
4. **Serve:**
   - Garnish with fresh parsley and serve immediately.

Spaghetti with Roasted Garlic and Parmesan

Ingredients:

- 400g spaghetti
- 1 head of garlic, roasted
- 1/4 cup olive oil
- 1/4 teaspoon red pepper flakes (optional)
- 1/2 cup Parmesan cheese, grated
- Salt and pepper to taste
- Fresh parsley for garnish

Instructions:

1. **Roast the Garlic:**
    - Preheat the oven to 375°F (190°C). Cut the top off a head of garlic and drizzle with olive oil. Wrap in foil and roast for 35-40 minutes until soft.
2. **Cook the Pasta:**
    - Cook spaghetti in salted boiling water until al dente. Drain and set aside.
3. **Make the Garlic Sauce:**
    - Squeeze the roasted garlic cloves out of their skins and mash into a paste. In a pan, heat olive oil and sauté the garlic paste for 1-2 minutes. Add red pepper flakes if desired.
4. **Combine:**
    - Toss cooked spaghetti with the garlic sauce, Parmesan cheese, salt, and pepper.
5. **Serve:**
    - Garnish with fresh parsley and serve immediately.

Shrimp and Pesto Stuffed Shells

Ingredients:

- 12 jumbo pasta shells
- 1 lb shrimp, peeled and deveined
- 1/2 cup basil pesto
- 1 cup ricotta cheese
- 1/2 cup mozzarella cheese, shredded
- 1/4 cup Parmesan cheese, grated
- Salt and pepper to taste
- 1 cup marinara sauce

Instructions:

1. **Cook the Pasta Shells:**
    - Cook the jumbo pasta shells in salted boiling water until al dente. Drain and set aside.
2. **Prepare the Shrimp:**
    - Sauté shrimp in a pan with olive oil until pink and cooked through. Chop shrimp into bite-sized pieces.
3. **Stuff the Shells:**
    - Mix pesto, ricotta, mozzarella, Parmesan, and chopped shrimp. Stuff each pasta shell with the mixture.
4. **Bake:**
    - Preheat oven to 375°F (190°C). Spread a thin layer of marinara sauce in a baking dish. Place stuffed shells on top, and cover with remaining marinara sauce. Bake for 20-25 minutes.
5. **Serve:**
    - Garnish with fresh basil and Parmesan before serving.

Spaghetti with Zucchini and Garlic

Ingredients:

- 400g spaghetti
- 2 medium zucchinis, thinly sliced
- 2 cloves garlic, minced
- 1/4 cup olive oil
- 1/4 teaspoon red pepper flakes (optional)
- Salt and pepper to taste
- Fresh basil for garnish

Instructions:

1. **Cook the Pasta:**
   - Cook spaghetti in salted boiling water until al dente. Drain and set aside.
2. **Sauté the Zucchini:**
   - In a pan, heat olive oil and sauté garlic for 1 minute. Add zucchini and cook for 5-7 minutes until softened. Season with salt, pepper, and red pepper flakes.
3. **Combine:**
   - Toss the cooked spaghetti with sautéed zucchini. Add more olive oil if necessary.
4. **Serve:**
   - Garnish with fresh basil and serve immediately.

Baked Rigatoni with Mozzarella and Basil

Ingredients:

- 400g rigatoni pasta
- 2 cups marinara sauce
- 1 1/2 cups mozzarella cheese, shredded
- 1/4 cup Parmesan cheese, grated
- 1/4 cup fresh basil, chopped
- Salt and pepper to taste

Instructions:

1. **Cook the Pasta:**
   - Cook rigatoni in salted boiling water until al dente. Drain and set aside.
2. **Assemble the Dish:**
   - Preheat the oven to 375°F (190°C). In a baking dish, mix cooked rigatoni with marinara sauce, mozzarella, and Parmesan cheese. Season with salt and pepper.
3. **Bake:**
   - Bake for 20-25 minutes until the cheese is melted and bubbly.
4. **Serve:**
   - Garnish with fresh basil before serving.

www.ingramcontent.com/pod-product-compliance
Lightning Source LLC
LaVergne TN
LVHW081343060526
838201LV00055B/2817